THIS LOGBOOK

BELONGS TO _____

Month 1 _____

Sun	Mon	Tue	Wed	Thu	Fri	Sat

Month 2 _____

Sun	Mon	Tue	Wed	Thu	Fri	Sat

Month 3 _____

Sun	Mon	Tue	Wed	Thu	Fri	Sat

Month 4 _____

Sun	Mon	Tue	Wed	Thu	Fri	Sat

Month 5 _____

Sun	Mon	Tue	Wed	Thu	Fri	Sat

Month 6 _____

Sun	Mon	Tue	Wed	Thu	Fri	Sat

Month 7 _____

Sun	Mon	Tue	Wed	Thu	Fri	Sat

Month 8 _____

Sun	Mon	Tue	Wed	Thu	Fri	Sat

Month 9 _____

Sun	Mon	Tue	Wed	Thu	Fri	Sat

Month 10 _____

Sun	Mon	Tue	Wed	Thu	Fri	Sat

Month 11 _____

Sun	Mon	Tue	Wed	Thu	Fri	Sat

Month 12_____

Sun	Mon	Tue	Wed	Thu	Fri	Sat

Table of Contents

Table of Contents

Grow

Strain Name _____ Seller _____ Price_____

Variety :Indica   Hybrid   Sativa   Color _____ Sex _____THC%_____CBD%_____

Grow From : _____   Room Type :_____

Date Started: _____   Purpose :   Flower   Edible   Concentrate

Week	Height	Light Schedule	Room Temperature	PH	Humidities	Nutrients	Notes

Date Harvested : _____

Grow it?   Easy   Normal   Hard   Resistance :   Strong   Neutral   Weak

Review

Date : _____   Week Harvested : _____

Strain Name _____ Seller _____ Price _____

Type :   Indica % _____   Sativa% _____   THC% _____ CBD% _____

Appearance _____

Method of consumption :   Vape   Smoke   Ingest

Tastes Like

Herbs
- ◯ Leaf
- ◯ Flowery

Fruity
- ◯ Citrus
- ◯ Berries
- ◯ Tropical

Earthy
- ◯ Sweet
- ◯ Spices
- ◯ Woody

Ferment
- ◯ Hops
- ◯ Cheese

Caustic
- ◯ Chemical

Effect

Positive		Negative
◯ Creative	◯ Energetic	◯ Dry Mouth
◯ Euphoric	◯ Happy	◯ Insomnia
◯ Relaxed	◯ Hungry	◯ Paranoia
◯ Sleep	◯ Talkative	◯ Dry Eyes
◯ Uplifted	◯ Giggly	

Duration _____

Notes.

_____

_____

Overall Rating   ☆ ☆ ☆ ☆ ☆

11

Grow

Strain Name _____ Seller _____ Price _____

Variety :Indica   Hybrid   Sativa   Color _____ Sex _____ THC%_____ CBD%_____

Grow From : _____   Room Type : _____

Date Started: _____   Purpose :   Flower   Edible   Concentrate

Week	Height	Light Schedule	Room Temperature	PH	Humidities	Nutrients	Notes

Date Harvested : _____

Grow it?   Easy   Normal   Hard   Resistance :   Strong   Neutral   Weak

Review

Date : _____   Week Harvested : _____

Strain Name _____ Seller _____ Price _____

Type :   Indica % _____   Sativa% _____   THC% _____ CBD% _____

Appearance _____

Method of consumption :   Vape   Smoke   Ingest

Tastes Like

Herbs
- ◯ Leaf
- ◯ Flowery

Fruity
- ◯ Citrus
- ◯ Berries
- ◯ Tropical

Earthy
- ◯ Sweet
- ◯ Spices
- ◯ Woody

Ferment
- ◯ Hops
- ◯ Cheese

Caustic
- ◯ Chemical

Effect

Positive		Negative
◯ Creative	◯ Energetic	◯ Dry Mouth
◯ Euphoric	◯ Happy	◯ Insomnia
◯ Relaxed	◯ Hungry	◯ Paranoia
◯ Sleep	◯ Talkative	◯ Dry Eyes
◯ Uplifted	◯ Giggly	

Duration _____

Notes.

_____

_____

Overall Rating ☆ ☆ ☆ ☆ ☆

Grow

Strain Name _____   Seller_____   Prioo_____

Variety :Indica   Hybrid   Sativa   Color _____   Sex _____THC%_____CBD%_____

Grow From : _____   Room Type :_____

Date Started: _____   Purpose :   Flower   Edible   Concentrate

Week	Height	Light Schedule	Room Temperature	PH	Humidities	Nutrients	Notes

Date Harvested : _____

Grow it?   Easy   Normal   Hard   Resistance :   Strong   Neutral   Weak

Review

Date : _____   Week Harvested : _____

Strain Name _____Seller_____ Price _____

Type :   Indica % _____ Sativa% _____   THC% _____ CBD% _____

Appearance _____

Method of consumption :   Vape   Smoke   Ingest

Tastes Like

Herbs
- ◯ Leaf
- ◯ Flowery

Fruity
- ◯ Citrus
- ◯ Berries
- ◯ Tropical

Earthy
- ◯ Sweet
- ◯ Spices
- ◯ Woody

Ferment
- ◯ Hops
- ◯ Cheese

Caustic
- ◯ Chemical

Effect

Positive		Negative
◯ Creative	◯ Energetic	◯ Dry Mouth
◯ Euphoric	◯ Happy	◯ Insomnia
◯ Relaxed	◯ Hungry	◯ Paranoia
◯ Sleep	◯ Talkative	◯ Dry Eyes
◯ Uplifted	◯ Giggly	

Duration _____

Notes.

_____

_____

Overall Rating ☆ ☆ ☆ ☆ ☆

Grow

Strain Name _____ Seller _____ Price_____

Variety : Indica Hybrid Sativa Color _____ Sex _____ THC%_____ CBD%_____

Grow From : _____ Room Type : _____

Date Started: _____ Purpose : Flower Edible Concentrate

Week	Height	Light Schedule	Room Temperature	PH	Humidities	Nutrients	Notes

Date Harvested : _____

Grow it? Easy   Normal   Hard   Resistance : Strong   Neutral   Weak

Review

Date : _____   Week Harvested : _____

Strain Name _____Seller _____Price _____

Type :   Indica % _____   Sativa% _____   THC% _____ CBD% _____

Appearance _____

Method of consumption :   Vape   Smoke   Ingest

Tastes Like

Herbs
- ○ Leaf
- ○ Flowery

Fruity
- ○ Citrus
- ○ Berries
- ○ Tropical

Earthy
- ○ Sweet
- ○ Spices
- ○ Woody

Ferment
- ○ Hops
- ○ Cheese

Caustic
- ○ Chemical

Effect

Positive		Negative
○ Creative	○ Energetic	○ Dry Mouth
○ Euphoric	○ Happy	○ Insomnia
○ Relaxed	○ Hungry	○ Paranoia
○ Sleep	○ Talkative	○ Dry Eyes
○ Uplifted	○ Giggly	

Duration _____

Notes.

_____

_____

Overall Rating ☆ ☆ ☆ ☆ ☆

Grow

Strain Name _____ Seller _____ Prioc _____

Variety : Indica Hybrid Sativa Color _____ Sex _____ THC% _____ CBD% _____

Grow From : _____ Room Type : _____

Date Started: _____ Purpose : Flower   Edible   Concentrate

Week	Height	Light Schedule	Room Temperature	PH	Humidities	Nutrients	Notes

Date Harvested : _____

Grow it? Easy   Normal   Hard   Resistance : Strong   Neutral   Weak

Review

Date : _____   Week Harvested : _____

Strain Name _____ Seller _____ Price _____

Type :   Indica % _____   Sativa% _____   THC% _____ CBD% _____

Appearance _____

Method of consumption :   Vape   Smoke   Ingest

Tastes Like

Herbs
- ◯ Leaf
- ◯ Flowery

Fruity
- ◯ Citrus
- ◯ Berries
- ◯ Tropical

Earthy
- ◯ Sweet
- ◯ Spices
- ◯ Woody

Ferment
- ◯ Hops
- ◯ Cheese

Caustic
- ◯ Chemical

Effect

Positive		Negative
◯ Creative	◯ Energetic	◯ Dry Mouth
◯ Euphoric	◯ Happy	◯ Insomnia
◯ Relaxed	◯ Hungry	◯ Paranoia
◯ Sleep	◯ Talkative	◯ Dry Eyes
◯ Uplifted	◯ Giggly	

Duration _____

Notes.

_____

_____

Overall Rating ☆ ☆ ☆ ☆ ☆

Grow

Strain Name _____ Seller _____ Price _____

Variety : Indica Hybrid Sativa Color _____ Sex _____ THC% _____ CBD% _____

Grow From : _____ Room Type : _____

Date Started: _____ Purpose : Flower Edible Concentrate

Week	Height	Light Schedule	Room Temperature	PH	Humidities	Nutrients	Notes

Date Harvested : _____

Grow it? Easy Normal Hard   Resistance : Strong Neutral Weak

20

Review

Date : _____   Week Harvested : _____

Strain Name _____ Seller _____ Price _____

Type :   Indica % _____   Sativa% _____   THC% _____ CBD% _____

Appearance _____

Method of consumption :   Vape   Smoke   Ingest

Tastes Like

Herbs
- ◯ Leaf
- ◯ Flowery

Fruity
- ◯ Citrus
- ◯ Berries
- ◯ Tropical

Earthy
- ◯ Sweet
- ◯ Spices
- ◯ Woody

Ferment
- ◯ Hops
- ◯ Cheese

Caustic
- ◯ Chemical

Effect

Positive		Negative
◯ Creative	◯ Energetic	◯ Dry Mouth
◯ Euphoric	◯ Happy	◯ Insomnia
◯ Relaxed	◯ Hungry	◯ Paranoia
◯ Sleep	◯ Talkative	◯ Dry Eyes
◯ Uplifted	◯ Giggly	

Duration _____

Notes.

_____

_____

Overall Rating ☆ ☆ ☆ ☆ ☆

Grow

Strain Name _____ Seller _____ Price_____

Variety : Indica   Hybrid   Sativa   Color _____ Sex _____THC%_____CBD%_____

Grow From : _____   Room Type : _____

Date Started: _____   Purpose :   Flower   Edible   Concentrate

Week	Height	Light Schedule	Room Temperature	PH	Humidities	Nutrients	Notes

Date Harvested : _____

Grow it?   Easy   Normal   Hard   Resistance :   Strong   Neutral   Weak

Review

Date : _____   Week Harvested : _____

Strain Name _____ Seller _____ Price _____

Type :   Indica % _____   Sativa% _____   THC% _____ CBD% _____

Appearance _____

Method of consumption :   Vape   Smoke   Ingest

Tastes Like

Herbs
- ◯ Leaf
- ◯ Flowery

Fruity
- ◯ Citrus
- ◯ Berries
- ◯ Tropical

Earthy
- ◯ Sweet
- ◯ Spices
- ◯ Woody

Ferment
- ◯ Hops
- ◯ Cheese

Caustic
- ◯ Chemical

Effect

Positive		Negative
◯ Creative	◯ Energetic	◯ Dry Mouth
◯ Euphoric	◯ Happy	◯ Insomnia
◯ Relaxed	◯ Hungry	◯ Paranoia
◯ Sleep	◯ Talkative	◯ Dry Eyes
◯ Uplifted	◯ Giggly	

Duration _____

Notes.

_____

_____

Overall Rating ☆ ☆ ☆ ☆ ☆

Grow

Strain Name _____ Seller _____ Prico _____

Variety : Indica   Hybrid   Sativa   Color _____ Sex _____ THC% _____ CBD% _____

Grow From : _____   Room Type : _____

Date Started: _____   Purpose :   Flower   Edible   Concentrate

Week	Height	Light Schedule	Room Temperature	PH	Humidities	Nutrients	Notes

Date Harvested : _____

Grow it?   Easy   Normal   Hard   Resistance :   Strong   Neutral   Weak

Review

Date : _____   Week Harvested : _____

Strain Name _____ Seller _____ Price _____

Type :   Indica % _____   Sativa% _____   THC% _____ CBD% _____

Appearance _____

Method of consumption :   Vape   Smoke   Ingest

Tastes Like

Herbs
- ◯ Leaf
- ◯ Flowery

Fruity
- ◯ Citrus
- ◯ Berries
- ◯ Tropical

Earthy
- ◯ Sweet
- ◯ Spices
- ◯ Woody

Ferment
- ◯ Hops
- ◯ Cheese

Caustic
- ◯ Chemical

Effect

Positive		Negative
◯ Creative	◯ Energetic	◯ Dry Mouth
◯ Euphoric	◯ Happy	◯ Insomnia
◯ Relaxed	◯ Hungry	◯ Paranoia
◯ Sleep	◯ Talkative	◯ Dry Eyes
◯ Uplifted	◯ Giggly	

Duration _____

Notes.

_____

_____

Overall Rating ☆ ☆ ☆ ☆ ☆

Grow

Strain Name _____ Seller_____ Prioc_____

Variety : Indica   Hybrid   Sativa   Color _____ Sex _____ THC%_____ CBD%_____

Grow From : _____   Room Type : _____

Date Started: _____   Purpose :   Flower   Edible   Concentrate

Week	Height	Light Schedule	Room Temperature	PH	Humidities	Nutrients	Notes

Date Harvested : _____

Grow it?   Easy   Normal   Hard   Resistance :   Strong   Neutral   Weak

Review

Date : _____   Week Harvested : _____

Strain Name _____ Seller _____ Price _____

Type :   Indica % _____   Sativa% _____   THC% _____ CBD% _____

Appearance _____

Method of consumption :   Vape   Smoke   Ingest

Tastes Like

Herbs
- ◯ Leaf
- ◯ Flowery

Fruity
- ◯ Citrus
- ◯ Berries
- ◯ Tropical

Earthy
- ◯ Sweet
- ◯ Spices
- ◯ Woody

Ferment
- ◯ Hops
- ◯ Cheese

Caustic
- ◯ Chemical

Effect

Positive		Negative
◯ Creative	◯ Energetic	◯ Dry Mouth
◯ Euphoric	◯ Happy	◯ Insomnia
◯ Relaxed	◯ Hungry	◯ Paranoia
◯ Sleep	◯ Talkative	◯ Dry Eyes
◯ Uplifted	◯ Giggly	

Duration _____

Notes.

_____

_____

Overall Rating ☆ ☆ ☆ ☆ ☆

Grow

Strain Name _____ Seller _____ Price

Variety : Indica   Hybrid   Sativa   Color _____ Sex _____ THC% _____ CBD% _____

Grow From : _____   Room Type : _____

Date Started: _____   Purpose :   Flower   Edible   Concentrate

Week	Height	Light Schedule	Room Temperature	PH	Humidities	Nutrients	Notes

Date Harvested : _____

Grow it?   Easy   Normal   Hard   Resistance :   Strong   Neutral   Weak

Review

Date : _____   Week Harvested : _____

Strain Name _____ Seller _____ Price _____

Type :   Indica % _____   Sativa% _____   THC% _____ CBD% _____

Appearance _____

Method of consumption :   Vape   Smoke   Ingest

Tastes Like

Herbs
- ◯ Leaf
- ◯ Flowery

Fruity
- ◯ Citrus
- ◯ Berries
- ◯ Tropical

Earthy
- ◯ Sweet
- ◯ Spices
- ◯ Woody

Ferment
- ◯ Hops
- ◯ Cheese

Caustic
- ◯ Chemical

Effect

Positive		Negative
◯ Creative	◯ Energetic	◯ Dry Mouth
◯ Euphoric	◯ Happy	◯ Insomnia
◯ Relaxed	◯ Hungry	◯ Paranoia
◯ Sleep	◯ Talkative	◯ Dry Eyes
◯ Uplifted	◯ Giggly	

Duration _____

Notes.

_____

_____

Overall Rating ☆ ☆ ☆ ☆ ☆

Grow

Strain Name _____   Seller_____   Price_____

Variety : Indica   Hybrid   Sativa   Color _____   Sex _____ THC%_____ CBD%_____

Grow From : _____   Room Type : _____

Date Started: _____   Purpose :   Flower   Edible   Concentrate

Week	Height	Light Schedule	Room Temperature	PH	Humidities	Nutrients	Notes

Date Harvested : _____

Grow it?   Easy   Normal   Hard   Resistance :   Strong   Neutral   Weak

Review

Date : _____ Week Harvested : _____

Strain Name _____ Seller _____ Price _____

Type : Indica % _____ Sativa% _____ THC% _____ CBD% _____

Appearance _____

Method of consumption : Vape Smoke Ingest

Tastes Like

Herbs
- ◯ Leaf
- ◯ Flowery

Ferment
- ◯ Hops
- ◯ Cheese

Fruity
- ◯ Citrus
- ◯ Berries
- ◯ Tropical

Caustic
- ◯ Chemical

Earthy
- ◯ Sweet
- ◯ Spices
- ◯ Woody

Effect

Positive		Negative
◯ Creative	◯ Energetic	◯ Dry Mouth
◯ Euphoric	◯ Happy	◯ Insomnia
◯ Relaxed	◯ Hungry	◯ Paranoia
◯ Sleep	◯ Talkative	◯ Dry Eyes
◯ Uplifted	◯ Giggly	

Duration _____

Notes.

_____

_____

Overall Rating ☆ ☆ ☆ ☆ ☆

Grow

Strain Name _____ Seller _____ Price _____

Variety : Indica Hybrid Sativa Color _____ Sex _____THC%_____CBD%_____

Grow From : _____ Room Type : _____

Date Started: _____ Purpose : Flower Edible Concentrate

Week	Height	Light Schedule	Room Temperature	PH	Humidities	Nutrients	Notes

Date Harvested : _____

Grow it? Easy   Normal   Hard   Resistance : Strong   Neutral   Weak

Review

Date : _____ Week Harvested : _____

Strain Name _____ Seller _____ Price _____

Type :   Indica % _____ Sativa% _____   THC% _____ CBD% _____

Appearance _____

Method of consumption :   Vape   Smoke   Ingest

Tastes Like

Herbs
- ○ Leaf
- ○ Flowery

Fruity
- ○ Citrus
- ○ Berries
- ○ Tropical

Earthy
- ○ Sweet
- ○ Spices
- ○ Woody

Ferment
- ○ Hops
- ○ Cheese

Caustic
- ○ Chemical

Effect

Positive		Negative
○ Creative	○ Energetic	○ Dry Mouth
○ Euphoric	○ Happy	○ Insomnia
○ Relaxed	○ Hungry	○ Paranoia
○ Sleep	○ Talkative	○ Dry Eyes
○ Uplifted	○ Giggly	

Duration _____

Notes.

_____

_____

Overall Rating ☆ ☆ ☆ ☆ ☆

Grow

Strain Name _____ Seller_____ Price_____

Variety :Indica Hybrid Sativa Color _____ Sex _____THC%_____CBD%_____

Grow From : _____ Room Type : _____

Date Started: _____ Purpose : Flower Edible Concentrate

Week	Height	Light Schedule	Room Temperature	PH	Humidities	Nutrients	Notes

Date Harvested : _____

Grow it? Easy   Normal   Hard   Resistance : Strong   Neutral   Weak

34

Review

Date : _____ Week Harvested : _____

Strain Name _____ Seller _____ Price _____

Type : Indica % _____ Sativa% _____ THC% _____ CBD% _____

Appearance _____

Method of consumption :   Vape   Smoke   Ingest

Tastes Like

Herbs
- ◯ Leaf
- ◯ Flowery

Fruity
- ◯ Citrus
- ◯ Berries
- ◯ Tropical

Earthy
- ◯ Sweet
- ◯ Spices
- ◯ Woody

Ferment
- ◯ Hops
- ◯ Cheese

Caustic
- ◯ Chemical

Effect

Positive		Negative
◯ Creative	◯ Energetic	◯ Dry Mouth
◯ Euphoric	◯ Happy	◯ Insomnia
◯ Relaxed	◯ Hungry	◯ Paranoia
◯ Sleep	◯ Talkative	◯ Dry Eyes
◯ Uplifted	◯ Giggly	

Duration _____

Notes.

_____

_____

Overall Rating ☆ ☆ ☆ ☆ ☆   35

Grow

Strain Name _____   Seller _____   Price _____

Variety : Indica   Hybrid   Sativa   Color _____   Sex _____ THC% _____ CBD% _____

Grow From : _____   Room Type : _____

Date Started: _____   Purpose :   Flower   Edible   Concentrate

Week	Height	Light Schedule	Room Temperature	PH	Humidities	Nutrients	Notes

Date Harvested : _____

Grow it?   Easy   Normal   Hard   Resistance :   Strong   Neutral   Weak

Review

Date : _____   Week Harvested : _____

Strain Name _____Seller _____ Price _____

Type :   Indica % _____   Sativa% _____   THC% _____ CBD% _____

Appearance _____

Method of consumption :   Vape   Smoke   Ingest

Tastes Like

Herbs
- ◯ Leaf
- ◯ Flowery

Fruity
- ◯ Citrus
- ◯ Berries
- ◯ Tropical

Earthy
- ◯ Sweet
- ◯ Spices
- ◯ Woody

Ferment
- ◯ Hops
- ◯ Cheese

Caustic
- ◯ Chemical

Effect

Positive		Negative
◯ Creative	◯ Energetic	◯ Dry Mouth
◯ Euphoric	◯ Happy	◯ Insomnia
◯ Relaxed	◯ Hungry	◯ Paranoia
◯ Sleep	◯ Talkative	◯ Dry Eyes
◯ Uplifted	◯ Giggly	

Duration _____

Notes.

_____

_____

Overall Rating ☆ ☆ ☆ ☆ ☆

Grow

Strain Name _____ Seller _____ Prico _____

Variety : Indica Hybrid Sativa Color _____ Sex _____ THC% _____ CBD% _____

Grow From : _____   Room Type : _____

Date Started: _____   Purpose : Flower   Edible   Concentrate

Week	Height	Light Schedule	Room Temperature	PH	Humidities	Nutrients	Notes

Date Harvested : _____

Grow it? Easy   Normal   Hard   Resistance : Strong   Neutral   Weak

Review

Date : _____   Week Harvested : _____

Strain Name _____ Seller _____ Price _____

Type :   Indica % _____   Sativa% _____   THC% _____ CBD% _____

Appearance _____

Method of consumption :   Vape   Smoke   Ingest

Tastes Like

Herbs
- ◯ Leaf
- ◯ Flowery

Fruity
- ◯ Citrus
- ◯ Berries
- ◯ Tropical

Earthy
- ◯ Sweet
- ◯ Spices
- ◯ Woody

Ferment
- ◯ Hops
- ◯ Cheese

Caustic
- ◯ Chemical

Effect

Positive		Negative
◯ Creative	◯ Energetic	◯ Dry Mouth
◯ Euphoric	◯ Happy	◯ Insomnia
◯ Relaxed	◯ Hungry	◯ Paranoia
◯ Sleep	◯ Talkative	◯ Dry Eyes
◯ Uplifted	◯ Giggly	

Duration _____

Notes.

_____

_____

Overall Rating ☆ ☆ ☆ ☆ ☆

39

Grow

Strain Name _____ Seller _____ Price

Variety : Indica Hybrid Sativa Color _____ Sex _____ THC% _____ CBD% _____

Grow From : _____ Room Type : _____

Date Started: _____ Purpose : Flower Edible Concentrate

Week	Height	Light Schedule	Room Temperature	PH	Humidities	Nutrients	Notes

Date Harvested : _____

Grow it? Easy   Normal   Hard   Resistance : Strong Neutral Weak

Review

Date : _____   Week Harvested : _____

Strain Name _____ Seller _____ Price _____

Type :   Indica % _____   Sativa% _____   THC% _____ CBD% _____

Appearance _____

Method of consumption :   Vape   Smoke   Ingest

Tastes Like

Herbs
- ◯ Leaf
- ◯ Flowery

Fruity
- ◯ Citrus
- ◯ Berries
- ◯ Tropical

Earthy
- ◯ Sweet
- ◯ Spices
- ◯ Woody

Ferment
- ◯ Hops
- ◯ Cheese

Caustic
- ◯ Chemical

Effect

Positive		Negative
◯ Creative	◯ Energetic	◯ Dry Mouth
◯ Euphoric	◯ Happy	◯ Insomnia
◯ Relaxed	◯ Hungry	◯ Paranoia
◯ Sleep	◯ Talkative	◯ Dry Eyes
◯ Uplifted	◯ Giggly	

Duration _____

Notes.

_____

_____

Overall Rating ☆ ☆ ☆ ☆ ☆

Grow

Strain Name _____ Seller_____ Prico_____

Variety : Indica Hybrid Sativa   Color _____ Sex _____ THC%_____ CBD%_____

Grow From :_____   Room Type :_____

Date Started: _____   Purpose : Flower   Edible   Concentrate

Week	Height	Light Schedule	Room Temperature	PH	Humidities	Nutrients	Notes

Date Harvested : _____

Grow it? Easy   Normal   Hard   Resistance : Strong   Neutral   Weak

Review

Date : _____   Week Harvested : _____

Strain Name _____ Seller _____ Price _____

Type : Indica % _____ Sativa% _____ THC% _____ CBD% _____

Appearance _____

Method of consumption :   Vape   Smoke   Ingest

Tastes Like

Herbs
- ◯ Leaf
- ◯ Flowery

Fruity
- ◯ Citrus
- ◯ Berries
- ◯ Tropical

Earthy
- ◯ Sweet
- ◯ Spices
- ◯ Woody

Ferment
- ◯ Hops
- ◯ Cheese

Caustic
- ◯ Chemical

Effect

Positive		Negative
◯ Creative	◯ Energetic	◯ Dry Mouth
◯ Euphoric	◯ Happy	◯ Insomnia
◯ Relaxed	◯ Hungry	◯ Paranoia
◯ Sleep	◯ Talkative	◯ Dry Eyes
◯ Uplifted	◯ Giggly	

Duration _____

Notes.

_____

_____

Overall Rating ☆ ☆ ☆ ☆ ☆   43

Grow

Strain Name _____ Seller_____ Price _____

Variety : Indica Hybrid Sativa Color _____ Sex _____ THC% _____ CBD% _____

Grow From : _____ Room Type : _____

Date Started: _____ Purpose : Flower Edible Concentrate

Week	Height	Light Schedule	Room Temperature	PH	Humidities	Nutrients	Notes

Date Harvested : _____

Grow it? Easy   Normal   Hard   Resistance : Strong   Neutral   Weak

Review

Date : _____   Week Harvested : _____

Strain Name _____Seller _____Price _____

Type :   Indica % _____ Sativa% _____   THC% _____ CBD% _____

Appearance _____

Method of consumption :   Vape   Smoke   Ingest

Tastes Like

Herbs
- ○ Leaf
- ○ Flowery

Fruity
- ○ Citrus
- ○ Berries
- ○ Tropical

Earthy
- ○ Sweet
- ○ Spices
- ○ Woody

Ferment
- ○ Hops
- ○ Cheese

Caustic
- ○ Chemical

Effect

Positive		Negative
○ Creative	○ Energetic	○ Dry Mouth
○ Euphoric	○ Happy	○ Insomnia
○ Relaxed	○ Hungry	○ Paranoia
○ Sleep	○ Talkative	○ Dry Eyes
○ Uplifted	○ Giggly	

Duration _____

Notes.

_____

_____

Overall Rating   ☆ ☆ ☆ ☆ ☆

Grow

Strain Name _____ Seller_____ Price _____

Variety : Indica Hybrid Sativa   Color _____ Sex _____ THC%_____CBD%_____

Grow From : _____   Room Type : _____

Date Started: _____   Purpose : Flower   Edible   Concentrate

Week	Height	Light Schedule	Room Temperature	PH	Humidities	Nutrients	Notes

Date Harvested : _____

Grow it? Easy   Normal   Hard   Resistance : Strong   Neutral   Weak

Review

Date : _____   Week Harvested : _____

Strain Name _____Seller _____Price _____

Type :   Indica % _____   Sativa% _____   THC% _____ CBD% _____

Appearance _____

Method of consumption :   Vape   Smoke   Ingest

Tastes Like

Herbs
- ◯ Leaf
- ◯ Flowery

Fruity
- ◯ Citrus
- ◯ Berries
- ◯ Tropical

Earthy
- ◯ Sweet
- ◯ Spices
- ◯ Woody

Ferment
- ◯ Hops
- ◯ Cheese

Caustic
- ◯ Chemical

Effect

Positive		Negative
◯ Creative	◯ Energetic	◯ Dry Mouth
◯ Euphoric	◯ Happy	◯ Insomnia
◯ Relaxed	◯ Hungry	◯ Paranoia
◯ Sleep	◯ Talkative	◯ Dry Eyes
◯ Uplifted	◯ Giggly	

Duration _____

Notes.

_____

_____

Overall Rating ☆ ☆ ☆ ☆ ☆

Grow

Strain Name _____ Seller _____ Price _____

Variety : Indica Hybrid Sativa Color _____ Sex _____ THC% _____ CBD% _____

Grow From : _____ Room Type : _____

Date Started: _____ Purpose : Flower   Edible   Concentrate

Week	Height	Light Schedule	Room Temperature	PH	Humidities	Nutrients	Notes

Date Harvested : _____

Grow it? Easy   Normal   Hard   Resistance : Strong   Neutral   Weak

Review

Date : _____   Week Harvested : _____

Strain Name _____ Seller _____ Price _____

Type :   Indica % _____   Sativa% _____   THC% _____ CBD% _____

Appearance _____

Method of consumption :   Vape   Smoke   Ingest

Tastes Like

Herbs
- ◯ Leaf
- ◯ Flowery

Fruity
- ◯ Citrus
- ◯ Berries
- ◯ Tropical

Earthy
- ◯ Sweet
- ◯ Spices
- ◯ Woody

Ferment
- ◯ Hops
- ◯ Cheese

Caustic
- ◯ Chemical

Effect

Positive		Negative
◯ Creative	◯ Energetic	◯ Dry Mouth
◯ Euphoric	◯ Happy	◯ Insomnia
◯ Relaxed	◯ Hungry	◯ Paranoia
◯ Sleep	◯ Talkative	◯ Dry Eyes
◯ Uplifted	◯ Giggly	

Duration _____

Notes.

_____

_____

Overall Rating ☆ ☆ ☆ ☆ ☆   49

Grow

Strain Name _____ Seller_____ Price_____

Variety : Indica   Hybrid   Sativa   Color _____ Sex _____THC%_____CBD%_____

Grow From : _____   Room Type : _____

Date Started: _____   Purpose :   Flower   Edible   Concentrate

Week	Height	Light Schedule	Room Temperature	PH	Humidities	Nutrients	Notes

Date Harvested : _____

Grow it?   Easy   Normal   Hard   Resistance :   Strong   Neutral   Weak

Review

Date : _____   Week Harvested : _____

Strain Name _____ Seller _____ Price _____

Type :   Indica % _____   Sativa% _____   THC% _____ CBD% _____

Appearance _____

Method of consumption :   Vape   Smoke   Ingest

Tastes Like

Herbs
- ○ Leaf
- ○ Flowery

Fruity
- ○ Citrus
- ○ Berries
- ○ Tropical

Earthy
- ○ Sweet
- ○ Spices
- ○ Woody

Ferment
- ○ Hops
- ○ Cheese

Caustic
- ○ Chemical

Effect

Positive		Negative
○ Creative	○ Energetic	○ Dry Mouth
○ Euphoric	○ Happy	○ Insomnia
○ Relaxed	○ Hungry	○ Paranoia
○ Sleep	○ Talkative	○ Dry Eyes
○ Uplifted	○ Giggly	

Duration _____

Notes.

_____

_____

Overall Rating ☆ ☆ ☆ ☆ ☆

Grow

Strain Name _____ Seller _____ Price _____

Variety : Indica Hybrid Sativa Color _____ Sex _____ THC% _____ CBD% _____

Grow From : _____ Room Type : _____

Date Started: _____ Purpose : Flower   Edible   Concentrate

Week	Height	Light Schedule	Room Temperature	PH	Humidities	Nutrients	Notes

Date Harvested : _____

Grow it? Easy   Normal   Hard   Resistance : Strong   Neutral   Weak

Review

Date : _____   Week Harvested : _____

Strain Name _____ Seller _____ Price _____

Type : Indica % _____ Sativa% _____   THC% _____ CBD% _____

Appearance _____

Method of consumption :   Vape   Smoke   Ingest

Tastes Like

Herbs
- ○ Leaf
- ○ Flowery

Fruity
- ○ Citrus
- ○ Berries
- ○ Tropical

Earthy
- ○ Sweet
- ○ Spices
- ○ Woody

Ferment
- ○ Hops
- ○ Cheese

Caustic
- ○ Chemical

Effect

Positive		Negative
○ Creative	○ Energetic	○ Dry Mouth
○ Euphoric	○ Happy	○ Insomnia
○ Relaxed	○ Hungry	○ Paranoia
○ Sleep	○ Talkative	○ Dry Eyes
○ Uplifted	○ Giggly	

Duration _____

Notes.

_____

_____

Overall Rating ☆ ☆ ☆ ☆ ☆

Grow

Strain Name _____ Seller _____ Price _____

Variety : Indica   Hybrid   Sativa   Color _____ Sex _____ THC% _____ CBD% _____

Grow From : _____ Room Type : _____

Date Started: _____ Purpose :   Flower   Edible   Concentrate

Week	Height	Light Schedule	Room Temperature	PH	Humidities	Nutrients	Notes

Date Harvested : _____

Grow it? Easy   Normal   Hard   Resistance : Strong   Neutral   Weak

Review

Date : _____   Week Harvested : _____

Strain Name _____ Seller _____ Price _____

Type :   Indica % _____   Sativa% _____   THC% _____ CBD% _____

Appearance _____

Method of consumption :   Vape   Smoke   Ingest

Tastes Like

Herbs
- ◯ Leaf
- ◯ Flowery

Fruity
- ◯ Citrus
- ◯ Berries
- ◯ Tropical

Earthy
- ◯ Sweet
- ◯ Spices
- ◯ Woody

Ferment
- ◯ Hops
- ◯ Cheese

Caustic
- ◯ Chemical

Effect

Positive		Negative
◯ Creative	◯ Energetic	◯ Dry Mouth
◯ Euphoric	◯ Happy	◯ Insomnia
◯ Relaxed	◯ Hungry	◯ Paranoia
◯ Sleep	◯ Talkative	◯ Dry Eyes
◯ Uplifted	◯ Giggly	

Duration _____

Notes.

_____

_____

Overall Rating ☆ ☆ ☆ ☆ ☆

55

Grow

Strain Name _____ Seller _____ Price _____

Variety : Indica   Hybrid   Sativa   Color _____   Sex _____ THC% _____ CBD% _____

Grow From : _____   Room Type : _____

Date Started: _____   Purpose :   Flower   Edible   Concentrate

Week	Height	Light Schedule	Room Temperature	PH	Humidities	Nutrients	Notes

Date Harvested : _____

Grow it?   Easy   Normal   Hard   Resistance :   Strong   Neutral   Weak

Review

Date : _____   Week Harvested : _____

Strain Name _____ Seller _____ Price _____

Type :   Indica % _____   Sativa% _____   THC% _____ CBD% _____

Appearance _____

Method of consumption :   Vape   Smoke   Ingest

Tastes Like

Herbs
- ○ Leaf
- ○ Flowery

Fruity
- ○ Citrus
- ○ Berries
- ○ Tropical

Earthy
- ○ Sweet
- ○ Spices
- ○ Woody

Ferment
- ○ Hops
- ○ Cheese

Caustic
- ○ Chemical

Effect

Positive		Negative
○ Creative	○ Energetic	○ Dry Mouth
○ Euphoric	○ Happy	○ Insomnia
○ Relaxed	○ Hungry	○ Paranoia
○ Sleep	○ Talkative	○ Dry Eyes
○ Uplifted	○ Giggly	

Duration _____

Notes.

_____

_____

Overall Rating ☆ ☆ ☆ ☆ ☆

Grow

Strain Name _____ Seller_____ Price_____

Variety : Indica Hybrid Sativa Color _____ Sex _____ THC%_____ CBD%_____

Grow From : _____ Room Type : _____

Date Started: _____ Purpose : Flower   Edible   Concentrate

Week	Height	Light Schedule	Room Temperature	PH	Humidities	Nutrients	Notes

Date Harvested : _____

Grow it? Easy   Normal   Hard   Resistance : Strong   Neutral   Weak

Review

Date : _____ Week Harvested : _____

Strain Name _____ Seller _____ Price _____

Type : Indica % _____ Sativa% _____ THC% _____ CBD% _____

Appearance _____

Method of consumption :   Vape   Smoke   Ingest

Tastes Like

Herbs
- ◯ Leaf
- ◯ Flowery

Fruity
- ◯ Citrus
- ◯ Berries
- ◯ Tropical

Earthy
- ◯ Sweet
- ◯ Spices
- ◯ Woody

Ferment
- ◯ Hops
- ◯ Cheese

Caustic
- ◯ Chemical

Effect

Positive		Negative
◯ Creative	◯ Energetic	◯ Dry Mouth
◯ Euphoric	◯ Happy	◯ Insomnia
◯ Relaxed	◯ Hungry	◯ Paranoia
◯ Sleep	◯ Talkative	◯ Dry Eyes
◯ Uplifted	◯ Giggly	

Duration _____

Notes.

_____

_____

Overall Rating ☆ ☆ ☆ ☆ ☆

Grow

Strain Name _____ Seller _____ Price _____

Variety : Indica   Hybrid   Sativa   Color _____ Sex _____ THC% _____ CBD% _____

Grow From : _____   Room Type : _____

Date Started: _____   Purpose :   Flower   Edible   Concentrate

Week	Height	Light Schedule	Room Temperature	PH	Humidities	Nutrients	Notes

Date Harvested : _____

Grow it?   Easy   Normal   Hard   Resistance :   Strong   Neutral   Weak

Review

Date : _____   Week Harvested : _____

Strain Name _____ Seller _____ Price _____

Type :   Indica % _____   Sativa% _____   THC% _____ CBD% _____

Appearance _____

Method of consumption :   Vape   Smoke   Ingest

Tastes Like

Herbs
- ○ Leaf
- ○ Flowery

Fruity
- ○ Citrus
- ○ Berries
- ○ Tropical

Earthy
- ○ Sweet
- ○ Spices
- ○ Woody

Ferment
- ○ Hops
- ○ Cheese

Caustic
- ○ Chemical

Effect

Positive		Negative
○ Creative	○ Energetic	○ Dry Mouth
○ Euphoric	○ Happy	○ Insomnia
○ Relaxed	○ Hungry	○ Paranoia
○ Sleep	○ Talkative	○ Dry Eyes
○ Uplifted	○ Giggly	

Duration _____

Notes.

_____

_____

Overall Rating ☆ ☆ ☆ ☆ ☆

Grow

Strain Name _____ Seller _____ Price _____

Variety : Indica Hybrid Sativa   Color _____   Sex _____ THC% _____ CBD% _____

Grow From : _____   Room Type : _____

Date Started: _____   Purpose : Flower   Edible   Concentrate

Week	Height	Light Schedule	Room Temperature	PH	Humidities	Nutrients	Notes

Date Harvested : _____

Grow it? Easy   Normal   Hard   Resistance : Strong   Neutral   Weak

Review

Date : _____ Week Harvested : _____

Strain Name _____ Seller _____ Price _____

Type : Indica % _____ Sativa% _____ THC% _____ CBD% _____

Appearance _____

Method of consumption :   Vape   Smoke   Ingest

Tastes Like

Herbs
- ◯ Leaf
- ◯ Flowery

Fruity
- ◯ Citrus
- ◯ Berries
- ◯ Tropical

Earthy
- ◯ Sweet
- ◯ Spices
- ◯ Woody

Ferment
- ◯ Hops
- ◯ Cheese

Caustic
- ◯ Chemical

Effect

Positive		Negative
◯ Creative	◯ Energetic	◯ Dry Mouth
◯ Euphoric	◯ Happy	◯ Insomnia
◯ Relaxed	◯ Hungry	◯ Paranoia
◯ Sleep	◯ Talkative	◯ Dry Eyes
◯ Uplifted	◯ Giggly	

Duration _____

Notes.

_____

_____

Overall Rating ☆ ☆ ☆ ☆ ☆   63

Grow

Strain Name _____ Seller _____ Price _____

Variety : Indica   Hybrid   Sativa   Color _____   Sex _____ THC%_____ CBD%_____

Grow From : _____   Room Type : _____

Date Started: _____   Purpose :   Flower   Edible   Concentrate

Week	Height	Light Schedule	Room Temperature	PH	Humidities	Nutrients	Notes

Date Harvested : _____

Grow it?   Easy   Normal   Hard   Resistance :   Strong   Neutral   Weak

Review

Date : _____   Week Harvested : _____

Strain Name _____ Seller _____ Price _____

Type :   Indica % _____   Sativa% _____   THC% _____ CBD% _____

Appearance _____

Method of consumption :   Vape   Smoke   Ingest

Tastes Like

Herbs
○ Leaf
○ Flowery

Fruity
○ Citrus
○ Berries
○ Tropical

Earthy
○ Sweet
○ Spices
○ Woody

Ferment
○ Hops
○ Cheese

Caustic
○ Chemical

Effect

Positive		Negative
○ Creative	○ Energetic	○ Dry Mouth
○ Euphoric	○ Happy	○ Insomnia
○ Relaxed	○ Hungry	○ Paranoia
○ Sleep	○ Talkative	○ Dry Eyes
○ Uplifted	○ Giggly	

Duration _____

Notes.

_____

_____

Overall Rating   ☆ ☆ ☆ ☆ ☆   65

Grow

Strain Name _____ Seller_____ Prioc_____

Variety :Indica Hybrid Sativa   Color _____ Sex_____THC%_____CBD%_____

Grow From :_____   Room Type :_____

Date Started: _____   Purpose : Flower   Edible   Concentrate

Week	Height	Light Schedule	Room Temperature	PH	Humidities	Nutrients	Notes

Date Harvested : _____

Grow it? Easy   Normal   Hard   Resistance : Strong   Neutral   Weak

Review

Date : _____   Week Harvested : _____

Strain Name _____ Seller _____ Price _____

Type :   Indica % _____   Sativa% _____   THC% _____ CBD% _____

Appearance _____

Method of consumption :   Vape   Smoke   Ingest

Tastes Like

Herbs
- ◯ Leaf
- ◯ Flowery

Fruity
- ◯ Citrus
- ◯ Berries
- ◯ Tropical

Earthy
- ◯ Sweet
- ◯ Spices
- ◯ Woody

Ferment
- ◯ Hops
- ◯ Cheese

Caustic
- ◯ Chemical

Effect

Positive		Negative
◯ Creative	◯ Energetic	◯ Dry Mouth
◯ Euphoric	◯ Happy	◯ Insomnia
◯ Relaxed	◯ Hungry	◯ Paranoia
◯ Sleep	◯ Talkative	◯ Dry Eyes
◯ Uplifted	◯ Giggly	

Duration _____

Notes.

_____

_____

Overall Rating ☆ ☆ ☆ ☆ ☆

Grow

Strain Name _____ Seller _____ Prioc _____

Variety : Indica Hybrid Sativa   Color _____ Sex _____ THC% _____ CBD% _____

Grow From : _____   Room Type : _____

Date Started: _____   Purpose :   Flower   Edible   Concentrate

Week	Height	Light Schedule	Room Temperature	PH	Humidities	Nutrients	Notes

Date Harvested : _____

Grow it? Easy   Normal   Hard   Resistance : Strong   Neutral   Weak

Review

Date : _____   Week Harvested : _____

Strain Name _____Seller_____ Price _____

Type : Indica % _____ Sativa% _____   THC% _____ CBD% _____

Appearance _____

Method of consumption :   Vape   Smoke   Ingest

Tastes Like

Herbs
- ◯ Leaf
- ◯ Flowery

Fruity
- ◯ Citrus
- ◯ Berries
- ◯ Tropical

Earthy
- ◯ Sweet
- ◯ Spices
- ◯ Woody

Ferment
- ◯ Hops
- ◯ Cheese

Caustic
- ◯ Chemical

Effect

Positive		Negative
◯ Creative	◯ Energetic	◯ Dry Mouth
◯ Euphoric	◯ Happy	◯ Insomnia
◯ Relaxed	◯ Hungry	◯ Paranoia
◯ Sleep	◯ Talkative	◯ Dry Eyes
◯ Uplifted	◯ Giggly	

Duration _____

Notes.

_____

_____

Overall Rating ☆ ☆ ☆ ☆ ☆

Grow

Strain Name _____ Seller _____ Price

Variety : Indica Hybrid Sativa   Color _____ Sex _____ THC% _____ CBD% _____

Grow From : _____   Room Type : _____

Date Started: _____   Purpose : Flower   Edible   Concentrate

Week	Height	Light Schedule	Room Temperature	PH	Humidities	Nutrients	Notes

Date Harvested : _____

Grow it? Easy   Normal   Hard   Resistance : Strong   Neutral   Weak

Review

Date : _____ Week Harvested : _____

Strain Name _____Seller _____ Price _____

Type : Indica % _____ Sativa% _____   THC% _____ CBD% _____

Appearance _____

Method of consumption :   Vape   Smoke   Ingest

Tastes Like

Herbs
- ◯ Leaf
- ◯ Flowery

Fruity
- ◯ Citrus
- ◯ Berries
- ◯ Tropical

Earthy
- ◯ Sweet
- ◯ Spices
- ◯ Woody

Ferment
- ◯ Hops
- ◯ Cheese

Caustic
- ◯ Chemical

Effect

Positive		Negative
◯ Creative	◯ Energetic	◯ Dry Mouth
◯ Euphoric	◯ Happy	◯ Insomnia
◯ Relaxed	◯ Hungry	◯ Paranoia
◯ Sleep	◯ Talkative	◯ Dry Eyes
◯ Uplifted	◯ Giggly	

Duration _____

Notes.

_____

_____

Overall Rating ☆ ☆ ☆ ☆ ☆   71

Grow

Strain Name _____ Seller _____ Price _____

Variety : Indica Hybrid Sativa Color _____ Sex _____ THC% _____ CBD% _____

Grow From : _____ Room Type : _____

Date Started: _____ Purpose : Flower   Edible   Concentrate

Week	Height	Light Schedule	Room Temperature	PH	Humidities	Nutrients	Notes

Date Harvested : _____

Grow it? Easy   Normal   Hard   Resistance : Strong   Neutral   Weak

Review

Date : _____ Week Harvested : _____

Strain Name _____ Seller _____ Price _____

Type :   Indica % _____ Sativa% _____   THC% _____ CBD% _____

Appearance _____

Method of consumption :   Vape   Smoke   Ingest

Tastes Like

Herbs
- Leaf
- Flowery

Fruity
- Citrus
- Berries
- Tropical

Earthy
- Sweet
- Spices
- Woody

Ferment
- Hops
- Cheese

Caustic
- Chemical

Effect

Positive		Negative
◯ Creative	◯ Energetic	◯ Dry Mouth
◯ Euphoric	◯ Happy	◯ Insomnia
◯ Relaxed	◯ Hungry	◯ Paranoia
◯ Sleep	◯ Talkative	◯ Dry Eyes
◯ Uplifted	◯ Giggly	

Duration _____

Notes.

_____

_____

Overall Rating ☆ ☆ ☆ ☆ ☆

Grow

Strain Name _____ Seller_____ Price_____

Variety : Indica Hybrid Sativa Color _____ Sex _____ THC%_____ CBD%_____

Grow From : _____ Room Type : _____

Date Started: _____ Purpose : Flower Edible Concentrate

Week	Height	Light Schedule	Room Temperature	PH	Humidities	Nutrients	Notes

Date Harvested : _____

Grow it? Easy   Normal   Hard   Resistance : Strong   Neutral   Weak

Review

Date : _____   Week Harvested : _____

Strain Name _____Seller _____ Price _____

Type :   Indica % _____   Sativa% _____   THC% _____ CBD% _____

Appearance _____

Method of consumption :   Vape   Smoke   Ingest

Tastes Like

Herbs
- ○ Leaf
- ○ Flowery

Fruity
- ○ Citrus
- ○ Berries
- ○ Tropical

Earthy
- ○ Sweet
- ○ Spices
- ○ Woody

Ferment
- ○ Hops
- ○ Cheese

Caustic
- ○ Chemical

Effect

Positive		Negative
○ Creative	○ Energetic	○ Dry Mouth
○ Euphoric	○ Happy	○ Insomnia
○ Relaxed	○ Hungry	○ Paranoia
○ Sleep	○ Talkative	○ Dry Eyes
○ Uplifted	○ Giggly	

Duration _____

Notes.

_____

_____

Overall Rating ☆ ☆ ☆ ☆ ☆

75

Grow

Strain Name _____ Seller _____ Prico _____

Variety : Indica Hybrid Sativa Color _____ Sex _____ THC% _____ CBD% _____

Grow From : _____ Room Type : _____

Date Started: _____ Purpose : Flower Edible Concentrate

Week	Height	Light Schedule	Room Temperature	PH	Humidities	Nutrients	Notes

Date Harvested : _____

Grow it? Easy   Normal   Hard   Resistance : Strong   Neutral   Weak

Review

Date : _____   Week Harvested : _____

Strain Name _____ Seller _____ Price _____

Type :   Indica % _____   Sativa% _____   THC% _____ CBD% _____

Appearance _____

Method of consumption :   Vape   Smoke   Ingest

Tastes Like

Herbs
- ◯ Leaf
- ◯ Flowery

Fruity
- ◯ Citrus
- ◯ Berries
- ◯ Tropical

Earthy
- ◯ Sweet
- ◯ Spices
- ◯ Woody

Ferment
- ◯ Hops
- ◯ Cheese

Caustic
- ◯ Chemical

Effect

Positive		Negative
◯ Creative	◯ Energetic	◯ Dry Mouth
◯ Euphoric	◯ Happy	◯ Insomnia
◯ Relaxed	◯ Hungry	◯ Paranoia
◯ Sleep	◯ Talkative	◯ Dry Eyes
◯ Uplifted	◯ Giggly	

Duration _____

Notes.

_____

_____

Overall Rating   ☆ ☆ ☆ ☆ ☆

Grow

Strain Name _____ Seller _____ Price _____

Variety : Indica Hybrid Sativa Color _____ Sex _____ THC% _____ CBD% _____

Grow From : _____ Room Type : _____

Date Started: _____ Purpose : Flower Edible Concentrate

Week	Height	Light Schedule	Room Temperature	PH	Humidities	Nutrients	Notes

Date Harvested : _____

Grow it? Easy   Normal   Hard   Resistance : Strong   Neutral   Weak

Review

Date : _____ Week Harvested : _____

Strain Name _____ Seller _____ Price _____

Type : Indica % _____ Sativa% _____ THC% _____ CBD% _____

Appearance _____

Method of consumption :   Vape   Smoke   Ingest

Tastes Like

Herbs
- ◯ Leaf
- ◯ Flowery

Fruity
- ◯ Citrus
- ◯ Berries
- ◯ Tropical

Earthy
- ◯ Sweet
- ◯ Spices
- ◯ Woody

Ferment
- ◯ Hops
- ◯ Cheese

Caustic
- ◯ Chemical

Effect

Positive		Negative
◯ Creative	◯ Energetic	◯ Dry Mouth
◯ Euphoric	◯ Happy	◯ Insomnia
◯ Relaxed	◯ Hungry	◯ Paranoia
◯ Sleep	◯ Talkative	◯ Dry Eyes
◯ Uplifted	◯ Giggly	

Duration _____

Notes.

_____

_____

Overall Rating ☆ ☆ ☆ ☆ ☆

Grow

Strain Name _____ Seller _____ Prioo _____

Variety : Indica   Hybrid   Sativa   Color _____   Sex _____ THC% _____ CBD% _____

Grow From : _____   Room Type : _____

Date Started: _____   Purpose :   Flower   Edible   Concentrate

Week	Height	Light Schedule	Room Temperature	PH	Humidities	Nutrients	Notes

Date Harvested : _____

Grow it? Easy   Normal   Hard   Resistance : Strong   Neutral   Weak

Review

Date : _____   Week Harvested : _____

Strain Name _____ Seller _____ Price _____

Type :   Indica % _____   Sativa% _____   THC% _____ CBD% _____

Appearance _____

Method of consumption :   Vape   Smoke   Ingest

Tastes Like

Herbs
- ◯ Leaf
- ◯ Flowery

Fruity
- ◯ Citrus
- ◯ Berries
- ◯ Tropical

Earthy
- ◯ Sweet
- ◯ Spices
- ◯ Woody

Ferment
- ◯ Hops
- ◯ Cheese

Caustic
- ◯ Chemical

Effect

Positive		Negative
◯ Creative	◯ Energetic	◯ Dry Mouth
◯ Euphoric	◯ Happy	◯ Insomnia
◯ Relaxed	◯ Hungry	◯ Paranoia
◯ Sleep	◯ Talkative	◯ Dry Eyes
◯ Uplifted	◯ Giggly	

Duration _____

Notes.

_____

_____

Overall Rating ☆ ☆ ☆ ☆ ☆

81

Grow

Strain Name _____ Seller _____ Prioo _____

Variety : Indica Hybrid Sativa   Color _____ Sex _____ THC% _____ CBD% _____

Grow From : _____   Room Type : _____

Date Started: _____   Purpose :   Flower   Edible   Concentrate

Week	Height	Light Schedule	Room Temperature	PH	Humidities	Nutrients	Notes

Date Harvested : _____

Grow it? Easy   Normal   Hard   Resistance : Strong   Neutral   Weak

Review

Date : _____   Week Harvested : _____

Strain Name _____ Seller _____ Price _____

Type :   Indica % _____   Sativa% _____   THC% _____ CBD% _____

Appearance _____

Method of consumption :   Vape   Smoke   Ingest

Tastes Like

Herbs
- ○ Leaf
- ○ Flowery

Fruity
- ○ Citrus
- ○ Berries
- ○ Tropical

Earthy
- ○ Sweet
- ○ Spices
- ○ Woody

Ferment
- ○ Hops
- ○ Cheese

Caustic
- ○ Chemical

Effect

Positive		Negative
○ Creative	○ Energetic	○ Dry Mouth
○ Euphoric	○ Happy	○ Insomnia
○ Relaxed	○ Hungry	○ Paranoia
○ Sleep	○ Talkative	○ Dry Eyes
○ Uplifted	○ Giggly	

Duration _____

Notes.

_____

_____

Overall Rating ☆ ☆ ☆ ☆ ☆

Grow

Strain Name _____ Seller _____ Price _____

Variety : Indica   Hybrid   Sativa   Color _____   Sex _____ THC% _____ CBD% _____

Grow From : _____   Room Type : _____

Date Started: _____   Purpose :   Flower   Edible   Concentrate

Week	Height	Light Schedule	Room Temperature	PH	Humidities	Nutrients	Notes

Date Harvested : _____

Grow it? Easy   Normal   Hard   Resistance :   Strong   Neutral   Weak

Review

Date : _____   Week Harvested : _____

Strain Name _____Seller _____Price _____

Type :   Indica % _____   Sativa% _____   THC% _____ CBD% _____

Appearance _____

Method of consumption :   Vape   Smoke   Ingest

Tastes Like

Herbs
- ◯ Leaf
- ◯ Flowery

Fruity
- ◯ Citrus
- ◯ Berries
- ◯ Tropical

Earthy
- ◯ Sweet
- ◯ Spices
- ◯ Woody

Ferment
- ◯ Hops
- ◯ Cheese

Caustic
- ◯ Chemical

Effect

Positive		Negative
◯ Creative	◯ Energetic	◯ Dry Mouth
◯ Euphoric	◯ Happy	◯ Insomnia
◯ Relaxed	◯ Hungry	◯ Paranoia
◯ Sleep	◯ Talkative	◯ Dry Eyes
◯ Uplifted	◯ Giggly	

Duration _____

Notes.

_____

_____

Overall Rating   ☆ ☆ ☆ ☆ ☆   85

Grow

Strain Name _____ Seller _____ Prioc _____

Variety : Indica   Hybrid   Sativa   Color _____   Sex _____ THC% _____ CBD% _____

Grow From : _____   Room Type : _____

Date Started: _____   Purpose :   Flower   Edible   Concentrate

Week	Height	Light Schedule	Room Temperature	PH	Humidities	Nutrients	Notes

Date Harvested : _____

Grow it? Easy   Normal   Hard   Resistance : Strong   Neutral   Weak

Review

Date : _____ Week Harvested : _____

Strain Name _____ Seller _____ Price _____

Type :   Indica % _____   Sativa% _____   THC% _____ CBD% _____

Appearance _____

Method of consumption :   Vape   Smoke   Ingest

Tastes Like

Herbs
- ◯ Leaf
- ◯ Flowery

Fruity
- ◯ Citrus
- ◯ Berries
- ◯ Tropical

Earthy
- ◯ Sweet
- ◯ Spices
- ◯ Woody

Ferment
- ◯ Hops
- ◯ Cheese

Caustic
- ◯ Chemical

Effect

Positive		Negative
◯ Creative	◯ Energetic	◯ Dry Mouth
◯ Euphoric	◯ Happy	◯ Insomnia
◯ Relaxed	◯ Hungry	◯ Paranoia
◯ Sleep	◯ Talkative	◯ Dry Eyes
◯ Uplifted	◯ Giggly	

Duration _____

Notes.

_____

_____

Overall Rating ☆ ☆ ☆ ☆ ☆

Grow

Strain Name _____   Seller_____   Price_____

Variety : Indica   Hybrid   Sativa   Color _____   Sex _____THC%_____CBD%_____

Grow From : _____   Room Type : _____

Date Started: _____   Purpose :   Flower   Edible   Concentrate

Week	Height	Light Schedule	Room Temperature	PH	Humidities	Nutrients	Notes

Date Harvested : _____

Grow it? Easy   Normal   Hard   Resistance : Strong   Neutral   Weak

Review

Date : _____   Week Harvested : _____

Strain Name _____ Seller _____ Price _____

Type :   Indica % _____   Sativa% _____   THC% _____ CBD% _____

Appearance _____

Method of consumption :   Vape   Smoke   Ingest

Tastes Like

Herbs
- ◯ Leaf
- ◯ Flowery

Fruity
- ◯ Citrus
- ◯ Berries
- ◯ Tropical

Earthy
- ◯ Sweet
- ◯ Spices
- ◯ Woody

Ferment
- ◯ Hops
- ◯ Cheese

Caustic
- ◯ Chemical

Effect

Positive		Negative
◯ Creative	◯ Energetic	◯ Dry Mouth
◯ Euphoric	◯ Happy	◯ Insomnia
◯ Relaxed	◯ Hungry	◯ Paranoia
◯ Sleep	◯ Talkative	◯ Dry Eyes
◯ Uplifted	◯ Giggly	

Duration _____

Notes.

_____

_____

Overall Rating ☆ ☆ ☆ ☆ ☆

Grow

Strain Name _____   Seller _____   Price _____

Variety : Indica Hybrid Sativa   Color _____   Sex _____ THC% _____ CBD% _____

Grow From : _____   Room Type : _____

Date Started: _____   Purpose : Flower   Edible   Concentrate

Week	Height	Light Schedule	Room Temperature	PH	Humidities	Nutrients	Notes

Date Harvested : _____

Grow it? Easy   Normal   Hard   Resistance : Strong   Neutral   Weak

Review

Date : _____   Week Harvested : _____

Strain Name _____Seller_____ Price _____

Type :   Indica % _____   Sativa% _____   THC% _____ CBD% _____

Appearance _____

Method of consumption :   Vape   Smoke   Ingest

Tastes Like

Herbs
- ○ Leaf
- ○ Flowery

Fruity
- ○ Citrus
- ○ Berries
- ○ Tropical

Earthy
- ○ Sweet
- ○ Spices
- ○ Woody

Ferment
- ○ Hops
- ○ Cheese

Caustic
- ○ Chemical

Effect

Positive		Negative
○ Creative	○ Energetic	○ Dry Mouth
○ Euphoric	○ Happy	○ Insomnia
○ Relaxed	○ Hungry	○ Paranoia
○ Sleep	○ Talkative	○ Dry Eyes
○ Uplifted	○ Giggly	

Duration _____

Notes.

_____

_____

Overall Rating ☆ ☆ ☆ ☆ ☆

91

Grow

Strain Name _____ Seller _____ Prioo _____

Variety : Indica Hybrid Sativa Color _____ Sex _____ THC% _____ CBD% _____

Grow From : _____ Room Type : _____

Date Started: _____ Purpose : Flower Edible Concentrate

Week	Height	Light Schedule	Room Temperature	PH	Humidities	Nutrients	Notes

Date Harvested : _____

Grow it? Easy   Normal   Hard   Resistance : Strong   Neutral   Weak

Review

Date : _____   Week Harvested : _____

Strain Name _____ Seller _____ Price _____

Type :   Indica % _____   Sativa% _____   THC% _____ CBD% _____

Appearance _____

Method of consumption :   Vape   Smoke   Ingest

Tastes Like

Herbs
- ◯ Leaf
- ◯ Flowery

Fruity
- ◯ Citrus
- ◯ Berries
- ◯ Tropical

Earthy
- ◯ Sweet
- ◯ Spices
- ◯ Woody

Ferment
- ◯ Hops
- ◯ Cheese

Caustic
- ◯ Chemical

Effect

Positive		Negative
◯ Creative	◯ Energetic	◯ Dry Mouth
◯ Euphoric	◯ Happy	◯ Insomnia
◯ Relaxed	◯ Hungry	◯ Paranoia
◯ Sleep	◯ Talkative	◯ Dry Eyes
◯ Uplifted	◯ Giggly	

Duration _____

Notes.

_____

_____

Overall Rating ☆ ☆ ☆ ☆ ☆

Grow

Strain Name _____ Seller _____ Price _____

Variety : Indica Hybrid Sativa Color _____ Sex _____ THC% _____ CBD% _____

Grow From : _____ Room Type : _____

Date Started: _____ Purpose : Flower Edible Concentrate

Week	Height	Light Schedule	Room Temperature	PH	Humidities	Nutrients	Notes

Date Harvested : _____

Grow it? Easy   Normal   Hard   Resistance : Strong   Neutral   Weak

Review

Date : _____   Week Harvested : _____

Strain Name _____Seller_____ Price _____

Type :   Indica % _____   Sativa% _____   THC% _____ CBD% _____

Appearance _____

Method of consumption :   Vape   Smoke   Ingest

Tastes Like

Herbs
- ◯ Leaf
- ◯ Flowery

Fruity
- ◯ Citrus
- ◯ Berries
- ◯ Tropical

Earthy
- ◯ Sweet
- ◯ Spices
- ◯ Woody

Ferment
- ◯ Hops
- ◯ Cheese

Caustic
- ◯ Chemical

Effect

Positive		Negative
◯ Creative	◯ Energetic	◯ Dry Mouth
◯ Euphoric	◯ Happy	◯ Insomnia
◯ Relaxed	◯ Hungry	◯ Paranoia
◯ Sleep	◯ Talkative	◯ Dry Eyes
◯ Uplifted	◯ Giggly	

Duration _____

Notes.

_____

_____

Overall Rating ☆ ☆ ☆ ☆ ☆   95

Grow

Strain Name _____   Seller _____   Price _____

Variety : Indica   Hybrid   Sativa   Color _____   Sex _____ THC% _____ CBD% _____

Grow From : _____   Room Type : _____

Date Started: _____   Purpose :   Flower   Edible   Concentrate

Week	Height	Light Schedule	Room Temperature	PH	Humidities	Nutrients	Notes

Date Harvested : _____

Grow it?   Easy   Normal   Hard   Resistance :   Strong   Neutral   Weak

Review

Date : _____   Week Harvested : _____

Strain Name _____ Seller _____ Price _____

Type :   Indica % _____   Sativa% _____   THC% _____ CBD% _____

Appearance _____

Method of consumption :   Vape   Smoke   Ingest

Tastes Like

Herbs
- ○ Leaf
- ○ Flowery

Fruity
- ○ Citrus
- ○ Berries
- ○ Tropical

Earthy
- ○ Sweet
- ○ Spices
- ○ Woody

Ferment
- ○ Hops
- ○ Cheese

Caustic
- ○ Chemical

Effect

Positive		Negative
○ Creative	○ Energetic	○ Dry Mouth
○ Euphoric	○ Happy	○ Insomnia
○ Relaxed	○ Hungry	○ Paranoia
○ Sleep	○ Talkative	○ Dry Eyes
○ Uplifted	○ Giggly	

Duration _____

Notes.

_____

_____

Overall Rating ☆ ☆ ☆ ☆ ☆

Grow

Strain Name _____ Seller _____ Price_____

Variety : Indica Hybrid Sativa Color _____ Sex _____THC%_____CBD%_____

Grow From : _____ Room Type : _____

Date Started: _____ Purpose : Flower Edible Concentrate

Week	Height	Light Schedule	Room Temperature	PH	Humidities	Nutrients	Notes

Date Harvested : _____

Grow it? Easy   Normal   Hard   Resistance : Strong   Neutral   Weak

Review

Date : _____   Week Harvested : _____

Strain Name _____Seller_____ Price _____

Type :   Indica % _____   Sativa% _____   THC% _____ CBD% _____

Appearance _____

Method of consumption :   Vape   Smoke   Ingest

Tastes Like

Herbs
- ◯ Leaf
- ◯ Flowery

Fruity
- ◯ Citrus
- ◯ Berries
- ◯ Tropical

Earthy
- ◯ Sweet
- ◯ Spices
- ◯ Woody

Ferment
- ◯ Hops
- ◯ Cheese

Caustic
- ◯ Chemical

Effect

Positive		Negative
◯ Creative	◯ Energetic	◯ Dry Mouth
◯ Euphoric	◯ Happy	◯ Insomnia
◯ Relaxed	◯ Hungry	◯ Paranoia
◯ Sleep	◯ Talkative	◯ Dry Eyes
◯ Uplifted	◯ Giggly	

Duration _____

Notes.

_____

_____

Overall Rating ☆ ☆ ☆ ☆ ☆

Grow

Strain Name _____ Seller _____ Price _____

Variety : Indica Hybrid Sativa Color _____ Sex _____ THC% _____ CBD% _____

Grow From : _____   Room Type : _____

Date Started: _____   Purpose :   Flower   Edible   Concentrate

Week	Height	Light Schedule	Room Temperature	PH	Humidities	Nutrients	Notes

Date Harvested : _____

Grow it? Easy   Normal   Hard   Resistance : Strong   Neutral   Weak

Review

Date : _____   Week Harvested : _____

Strain Name _____Seller _____Price _____

Type :   Indica % _____ Sativa% _____   THC% _____ CBD% _____

Appearance _____

Method of consumption :   Vape   Smoke   Ingest

Tastes Like

Herbs
- ○ Leaf
- ○ Flowery

Fruity
- ○ Citrus
- ○ Berries
- ○ Tropical

Earthy
- ○ Sweet
- ○ Spices
- ○ Woody

Ferment
- ○ Hops
- ○ Cheese

Caustic
- ○ Chemical

Effect

Positive		Negative
○ Creative	○ Energetic	○ Dry Mouth
○ Euphoric	○ Happy	○ Insomnia
○ Relaxed	○ Hungry	○ Paranoia
○ Sleep	○ Talkative	○ Dry Eyes
○ Uplifted	○ Giggly	

Duration _____

Notes.

_____

_____

Overall Rating   ☆ ☆ ☆ ☆ ☆

101

Grow

Strain Name _____ Seller _____ Price _____

Variety : Indica Hybrid Sativa   Color _____   Sex _____ THC% _____ CBD% _____

Grow From : _____   Room Type : _____

Date Started: _____   Purpose :   Flower   Edible   Concentrate

Week	Height	Light Schedule	Room Temperature	PH	Humidities	Nutrients	Notes

Date Harvested : _____

Grow it? Easy   Normal   Hard   Resistance : Strong   Neutral   Weak

Review

Date : _____   Week Harvested : _____

Strain Name _____Seller _____ Price _____

Type :   Indica % _____ Sativa% _____   THC% _____ CBD% _____

Appearance _____

Method of consumption :   Vape   Smoke   Ingest

Tastes Like

Herbs
- ◯ Leaf
- ◯ Flowery

Fruity
- ◯ Citrus
- ◯ Berries
- ◯ Tropical

Earthy
- ◯ Sweet
- ◯ Spices
- ◯ Woody

Ferment
- ◯ Hops
- ◯ Cheese

Caustic
- ◯ Chemical

Effect

Positive		Negative
◯ Creative	◯ Energetic	◯ Dry Mouth
◯ Euphoric	◯ Happy	◯ Insomnia
◯ Relaxed	◯ Hungry	◯ Paranoia
◯ Sleep	◯ Talkative	◯ Dry Eyes
◯ Uplifted	◯ Giggly	

Duration _____

Notes.

_____

_____

Overall Rating ☆ ☆ ☆ ☆ ☆   103

Grow

Strain Name _____ Seller_____ Prico_____

Variety : Indica   Hybrid   Sativa   Color _____   Sex _____ THC% _____ CBD% _____

Grow From : _____   Room Type : _____

Date Started: _____   Purpose :   Flower   Edible   Concentrate

Week	Height	Light Schedule	Room Temperature	PH	Humidities	Nutrients	Notes

Date Harvested : _____

Grow it?   Easy   Normal   Hard   Resistance :   Strong   Neutral   Weak

Review

Date : _____ Week Harvested : _____

Strain Name _____ Seller _____ Price _____

Type : Indica % _____ Sativa% _____ THC% _____ CBD% _____

Appearance _____

Method of consumption :   Vape   Smoke   Ingest

Tastes Like

Herbs
- ⭕ Leaf
- ⭕ Flowery

Fruity
- ⭕ Citrus
- ⭕ Berries
- ⭕ Tropical

Earthy
- ⭕ Sweet
- ⭕ Spices
- ⭕ Woody

Ferment
- ⭕ Hops
- ⭕ Cheese

Caustic
- ⭕ Chemical

Effect

Positive		Negative
⭕ Creative	⭕ Energetic	⭕ Dry Mouth
⭕ Euphoric	⭕ Happy	⭕ Insomnia
⭕ Relaxed	⭕ Hungry	⭕ Paranoia
⭕ Sleep	⭕ Talkative	⭕ Dry Eyes
⭕ Uplifted	⭕ Giggly	

Duration _____

Notes.

_____

_____

Overall Rating ☆ ☆ ☆ ☆ ☆

Grow

Strain Name _____   Seller_____   Prioo _____

Variety : Indica   Hybrid   Sativa   Color _____   Sex _____ THC% _____ CBD% _____

Grow From : _____   Room Type : _____

Date Started: _____   Purpose :   Flower   Edible   Concentrate

Week	Height	Light Schedule	Room Temperature	PH	Humidities	Nutrients	Notes

Date Harvested : _____

Grow it?   Easy   Normal   Hard   Resistance :   Strong   Neutral   Weak

Review

Date : _____   Week Harvested : _____

Strain Name _____Seller _____ Price _____

Type :   Indica % _____   Sativa% _____   THC% _____ CBD% _____

Appearance _____

Method of consumption :   Vape   Smoke   Ingest

Tastes Like

Herbs
- ◯ Leaf
- ◯ Flowery

Fruity
- ◯ Citrus
- ◯ Berries
- ◯ Tropical

Earthy
- ◯ Sweet
- ◯ Spices
- ◯ Woody

Ferment
- ◯ Hops
- ◯ Cheese

Caustic
- ◯ Chemical

Effect

Positive		Negative
◯ Creative	◯ Energetic	◯ Dry Mouth
◯ Euphoric	◯ Happy	◯ Insomnia
◯ Relaxed	◯ Hungry	◯ Paranoia
◯ Sleep	◯ Talkative	◯ Dry Eyes
◯ Uplifted	◯ Giggly	

Duration _____

Notes.

_____

_____

Overall Rating ☆ ☆ ☆ ☆ ☆

Grow

Strain Name _____ Seller _____ Price _____

Variety : Indica Hybrid Sativa Color _____ Sex _____ THC% _____ CBD% _____

Grow From : _____ Room Type : _____

Date Started: _____ Purpose : Flower   Edible   Concentrate

Week	Height	Light Schedule	Room Temperature	PH	Humidities	Nutrients	Notes

Date Harvested : _____

Grow it? Easy   Normal   Hard   Resistance : Strong   Neutral   Weak

Review

Date : _____   Week Harvested : _____

Strain Name _____Seller_____Price _____

Type :   Indica % _____   Sativa% _____   THC% _____ CBD% _____

Appearance _____

Method of consumption :   Vape   Smoke   Ingest

Tastes Like

Herbs
- ◯ Leaf
- ◯ Flowery

Fruity
- ◯ Citrus
- ◯ Berries
- ◯ Tropical

Earthy
- ◯ Sweet
- ◯ Spices
- ◯ Woody

Ferment
- ◯ Hops
- ◯ Cheese

Caustic
- ◯ Chemical

Effect

Positive		Negative
◯ Creative	◯ Energetic	◯ Dry Mouth
◯ Euphoric	◯ Happy	◯ Insomnia
◯ Relaxed	◯ Hungry	◯ Paranoia
◯ Sleep	◯ Talkative	◯ Dry Eyes
◯ Uplifted	◯ Giggly	

Duration _____

Notes.

_____

_____

Overall Rating ☆ ☆ ☆ ☆ ☆

NOTES

Made in United States
Troutdale, OR
12/14/2023